To Chip &
Ellen,
Enjoy the book
Joe

THE
SURFMASTER
A TALE OF LOVE AND HOPE

JOE COLANTUONI

COVER ILLUSTRATION:
ANNETTE COLANTUONI

Outskirts Press, Inc.
Denver, Colorado

The Surfmaster
A Tale of Love and Hope
Cover Illustration: Annette Colantuoni

Outskirts Press
http://www.outskirtspress.com

ISBN-10: 1-59800-403-4
ISBN-13: 978-1-59800-403-8

Outskirts Press and the "OP" logo are trademarks belonging to
Outskirts Press, Inc.

Printed in the United States of America

To all who believe in the power of
Faith, Hope and Love

THE MEETING

What was going on?

The mist that I had just walked through was so thick that I could not see my hand in front of me. As I breathed, my lungs filled with the moist heavy air. I could feel the heaviness in my diaphragm. This was beginning to freak me out. I went from a sparkling sunny award winning day to an oppressive gray green mist. If I could not feel the crunch of the sand beneath my feet, I'm sure I would have gone into a complete panic attack.

I trudged through what seemed like an eternity but I'm sure if I checked my watch (if I was even wearing one), it would have been only a few minutes.

My perseverance paid off and I stepped out of the mist -- back into a beautiful day -- at the point where the ocean and sand vie in eternal conflict.

About 10 yards in front of me, I glimpsed a lone surf fisherman. I thought that I needed to talk to him -- see what gear he's using, what if anything he's caught.

My wife Annette and I had spoken many times about spending time on the beach, surf fishing and just being together. And maybe we will, if she'll even talk to me after the way I act.

I know!

I'll try and get some good hints from this guy that I'm approaching and then shock Annette with my new found knowledge and all will be right again.

As I approached the fisherman, I started practicing in my mind how I would start up the conversation with him and how I would pick his brain.

I was about 3 feet from him when he turned away from the ocean towards me. He looked <u>directly</u> in my eyes. I was startled by this presumptuous act on his part, but a bigger shock was coming my way.

He said,

   "Joe, I've been waiting for you."

Whoa!! What was this? He knew my name? He was waiting for me?

I turned to go back where I came from.

   "Please stay, we need to talk", he said.

_____

Just 45 minutes ago, I was agitated and self absorbed.

There I was again -- upset!!! Marching down the outside steps.

What's wrong with them?   Don't they see how important I am to the family?

It's always the same. I want peace, love and happiness but then I do something to push their buttons. I try but fail miserably to be what I have quested my whole life for -- a person full of love and hope. Whenever it appears that I am on the right track, I say or do something to set me or my family back.

I decided to drive the two blocks to the beach. I opened the door to the car and sat behind the wheel.   The steering wheel felt smooth in my hands. I turned the key in the ignition and the engine began to hum. Why couldn't life be this easy? Turn the key -- happiness, -- turn the key -- love, -- turn the key -- peace.

Peace -- what an illusion. The world was in real trouble. War, famine and all sorts of problems. How could love survive in the current world situation?

Well, I'm not sure there was anything, I could do to help the world -- I often felt I couldn't even keep peace in my own family or even worse in my own mind.

It was an award winning day. The bluest of skies. Scarcely a cloud. And the temperature -- 73 degrees and this is December 3.

The gal on the Weather Channel said that we had already broken the record and this was only 1PM.

Why didn't I become a Weather Guy? Got to be one of the best gigs -- you can be wrong about your job 60% of the time and still keep it. Probably the only other job where you can connect with an even lower percentage and be considered a star is Major League Baseball -- its just not fair -- when I ran Payroll, accuracy had to be 99.8% or better -- and I didn't make a tenth of what the benchwarmers do -- Oh well!

Maybe I'm just a little too tightly wound today. This time with the warmth of the sun and the rhythm of the waves should serve to loosen my spirit some. It's always helped in the past. Though admittedly, I haven't been this bad for a long time, if ever!

I opened the VW door and stepped out. The rays of the sun immediately warmed the skin on my face. And that ocean air -- clean, salty, distinctly fresh. I inhaled deeply and was exhilarated. I turned and pressed the remote lock, heard the car beep and turned to the dunes.

The tall beach grass gently swayed in the wind alongside the sandy path to the beach. The ocean glistened and sparkled, radiating the sun rays. The waves gently kissed the sandy shoreline. The hurricanes and nor'easter's had taken their toll on the beach. Where there formally had been 200 plus feet of sand, now at low tide, there was scarcely a hundred feet of beach.

Those times were past and now there was the beauty of this most wonderful day. I decided to walk towards the north.

The beach was alive with activity. A day like this can do that. There were solitary figures walking and thinking. There were families joking and running. There were dogs chasing whatever was thrown. The ocean air and the beach could bring out the best in people.

My mind was settling down. As I walked, I began to think. Is it just me or are humans in general programmed to mess up even the best of circumstances? I'm sure I appear to many as someone who has everything. But if I am, then why do I torture myself? Even worse why do I hurt those that I love? Wasn't there an old song about hurting the one you love? Could it be that humans just don't know how to be happy? Or how to really love?

As I continued walking, I noticed a thick mist developing about one hundred yards north of me. I debated whether to continue walking but decided that those I left at home would probably be glad if I stayed away a little longer.

Will I finally make them fed up with me? Will I finally push those I love so far away from me that I will be destined to die a lonely bitter soul? I need help - - I really do.

The mist was even closer now.

I continued walking and thinking.

I took another step and entered the mist.

"We need to talk!"-- What kind of scam is this? What does he mean?

Sure I'm originally from Brooklyn and have dealt with wiser guys and weirder circumstances than this -- or have I? No, I'm not going to let this guy ruin such a gorgeous day.

I bet it was just a lucky guess on the name. I'll show him I can't be rattled. I'll say something clever to show him I don't spook so easy -- even if his comment has rattled me a tad.

'So remember Fredo in the Godfather II? He said Hail Mary's when he wanted to catch fish -- you have any little words you say?'

"That part did amuse me -- I've said a few of them myself over the years -- they've worked for fish and lots of other things."

'So Buddy, you look like you're engrossed in what you're doin?'
"Sure am."
'You know you startled me a bit -- How'd you know my name?'
"I've seen you around."
'Oh, I guess you saw me at the library? Was that it?'
"Sure there and some other places."

I had started working in the library about two months ago. I had met many locals there -- that probably was how he knew my name. So far working at the library has been a gas -- I'm a lifetime student -- love to learn new things -- and this is the first low stress job that I have had in over 30 years.

I noticed that the fisherman had reeled in his line and was now looking into his tackle box. I waited a bit, not wanting to break his concentration. Then I said:

'Come here often?'

"Sure do."
'Mind if I hang here with you for a bit and watch?'
"Whatever you want -- I'm here and wouldn't mind some company -- remember we need to talk.'

Oh yeah -- that's right -- he wants to talk to me.

What could he have to say to me?

_____

I guess my first impression of this guy was all wrong. He now seemed to me just a regular guy who likes to spend some time near the ocean.

I was probably being too judgmental. I need to mellow out and start taking things slowly.

I sized this guy up and down. He looked kind of regular. He was about as best I could estimate about 5 foot 10 inches tall. Though it was hard to tell his exact weight with what he was wearing, he appeared to weigh about 180 pounds. He looked like he was in pretty good shape. It was hard to figure out his age though I assumed that he probably was about my age or a little older. He possessed no distinguishing characteristics -- he just appeared like anyone I might find at this time of year on the beach.

When I looked closer at him, I could see that he was a striking individual -- intense and peaceful. His voice possessed an air of authority. I felt like I could learn something from him.

He obviously was in his element at the surfline. He seemed to have all the equipment necessary to master anything that the surf might throw or gently hand over to him.

He was not just a surf fisherman -- to me, he was a surfmaster.

'So have you caught anything so far?'

"Had a couple of bites but nothing serious yet."

'How long you been out here?'

"Not all that long -- I'm glad you came around when you did."

'Why's that?'

"You'll see."

What the heck does that mean? I'll see

-- there I go again jumping at just about everything.

Probably just his way of talking -- I'm sure he means nothing by it.

He turned to me.

> "You know the worst thing you can do is try to make things happen before they're ready to. When the fish are ready, I'll catch them and if they're not -- well it'll be just a great day in the sun -- do you know what I mean?"

Did I know what he means? Sure, I think I do. Like when I try to make things happen and it ends in disaster. Then there are the other times when I stay out of the way and things just fall into place -- you know I'd rather be lucky than good.

What's with me? Why all this introspection? And on such a great day?

'So you think today might be a
fish day or just a sun day?'
"You know, Joe, I'm not sure, but
whichever I'll be ready."

———————————————

I sat silently for a few minutes, just in-haling the salty air. Luxuriating in the warmth of the sun, I felt renewed.

Now, I just couldn't wait to get back home.

I stood up and turned to the surfmaster.

'You know I think its time for me to go home.'

"Well, Joe, thanks for spending some time with me. You know the weather forecast is for another beautiful day tomorrow. I'll be here again -- if you come back, I'll show you how to cast and we can continue talking -- there really is more we need to talk about."

'That sounds great -- I have a bunch of things I need to do but I'll see if I can get back down here -- what time will you be here?'

"Oh, most of the day."

'Great -- see ya.'

With these last words, I turned and headed back up the beach. I felt much lighter inside. I felt a buoyancy that I had only felt for a fleeting few moments in my life.

_____

When I returned home, it was as if there had not been an emotional storm. As I turned the doorknob and opened the front door to enter the house, I was met with the most appetizing of aromas. Annette was cooking. The house was alive with the sweet smells of her efforts. Letting my nose do its detective work, I knew that Annette was making her fantastic sauce. There was also a smell of fried meat so I further deduced that I was going to be lucky and have her famous meatballs.

I entered the kitchen and there she was -- she smiled and gave me a hug.

> "What have you been up to?" she said.
> 'I went down to the beach to cool off -- I know I'm a jerk. I promise that I'll get it right one of these days.'
> "I know you will."

'I met a really interesting guy on the beach. He was surfcasting. He really seemed to know what he's doing.'

"What's his name?"

'You know I didn't get it -- I know, I know -- if it were you, you would have known his name, how old he was, if he was married, where he lived and the names of his kids!! I'm not good at that kind of stuff. But I do have a nickname for him!'

"What's that?"

'The Surfmaster.'

"Cool!"

'So what are we having for dinner? I smell some really great stuff.'

"Well, I made sauce, meatballs and eggplant parmigiana -- what kind of pasta do you want?"

'How about the one with the lines?'

"I'll see if I have any."

Joe, our son, was out on the deck having a smoke. When he came back in, he said,

"Hey big guy -- how you doin?"

And gave me that great big smile of his.

I opened a bottle of Chianti to go with this feast. Everything was superb as usual.

Our world was back in the groove.

_____

I could not sleep that night. The meeting with the stranger on the beach -- the Surfmaster -- was on my mind. I tossed and turned. No matter how hard I tried, I could not erase from my brain the words of the Surfmaster -- 'We need to talk'.

When I closed my eyes, I could see his image on the back of my eyelids.

What did he want to say? Why me?

I could not stop my mind from racing. Over and over, these thoughts assaulted my consciousness.

As soon as the sun rose, I dressed and went down to the beach. The overnight temperatures had dropped. The moist warm air from the ocean met the cooled down air from the land. I found myself once again in a mist.

Not feeling disturbed or concerned at all

that I could not see what was going on in front of me, I trudged on. At a distance, I could see a figure shrouded in fog. I continued and there in front of me was my new found acquaintance -- the Surfmaster.

I said,

'Good morning.'
"Good morning to you too, Joe."
'You're here awfully early.'
"Well you know the early bird catches the worm and oftentimes more than that. You're pretty early yourself. I thought you had some things to do this morning."
'I do but I guess I was a little anxious to continue our talk.'
"No need to be anxious. I told you I'd be here most of the day. You need to take care of those things that you had planned to do. I should be here later."
'Well, what if you're not?'
"Then I won't be -- that will mean

we were not supposed to talk anymore. But you know, I think we'll meet again. So go ahead get going."

After I left the beach, I went to the shopping market, then to the Post Office and then I checked to see how my mother was doing.

We moved to the beach a little over a year ago -- Annette, Joe, and my mom and dad. At first, the only wrinkle was leaving our baby Amanda back in Northern Virginia. Well baby is a stretch -- she was 24, had graduated from college and had a great job. But she'll always be our baby.

Before long, we had to face the most serious issue that humans are ever asked to deal with -- the fatal illness of a loved one. My dad passed away after only 5 months at the beach.

It had now been almost a year since my dad died but I was still worried about my mom. She was doing better than I had expected but I was still concerned.

They had been married over 58 years and it was tough for her to be alone. Many times, I asked her to move in with us but I think she still liked her independence.

When she opened the door, she looked great. I asked her to come over later that day and she said that sounded good.

I then brought my packages home and headed right back to the beach. I parked my car at the top of 136th Street and walked over the dunes.

Well, it was still a pretty nice day -- not as awesome as yesterday but still pretty darn good. Walking more unconsciously than usual, I reached the shore line and turned left heading north.

I walked and walked. I noticed that the odd mist from yesterday and this morning was no longer around.

I continued walking I'm sure longer

than my last two beach walks -- and to my disappointment, I did not see the Surfmaster in front of me.

Somewhat disillusioned, I started to consider going home. What if I would never see him again? I'm not sure I could deal with not knowing what the mysterious stranger wanted to tell me. Just then, the wind direction began to change. About 20 yards ahead of me, I noticed a mist, similar to what I walked through yesterday and this morning, begin to develop.

I walked a little further. When I did, I was pleasantly surprised to see my Surfmaster walk over the dune.

As soon as I saw him, I began to walk towards him. I waved my right hand and saw him wave back. Maybe I would be lucky and find out more about the Surfmaster on this third meeting.

"How you doin, Joe?"

'Great, I thought I missed you.'
"Well, you didn't. Now that you're here, I want to ask you something."
'Go ahead ask.'
"Are you happy?"

What kind of a question was that? And why does he care?

Even though I was a bit put back by the question -- I blurted out an answer.

'Sure I am.'
"Well that's great Joe, you know you have everything you need to be happy."

_____

I knew what he said was true -- but?

> "Joe, you have had a very wonderful life!"
> 'How do you know? We just met.'
> "No, Joe -- we have known each other for a very long time. You have not always seen me -- but I have been watching you -- and the whole world."

The hairs on the back of my neck began to dance. I started feeling that maybe I really did not understand who I was dealing with. The Surfmaster must have sensed my growing alarm because he said,

> "Joe, don't worry. I'm here to help you and the rest of the world but first there are a few things that you need to see."

He raised both arms up and the wind began to howl. The sand began swirling in the air. Soon I could hardly see the Surfmaster in front of me. The sound of the wind was howling in my ear. The noise rose to a deafening level. I could no longer hear my heart beat and just when I thought that my body would shake apart from the combined internal fear and the buffeting of the wind -- it stopped.

The Surfmaster looked at me and said,

> "Joe, lets first start with your life!"

_____

THE REVIEW

And there we were standing on the beach and looking at past events of my life.

I observed my life as if I was watching a movie -- but I knew all the characters and how each scene would play out.

There was no temporal order to the unwinding of the plot of my life.

He wanted to make a point -- and that's why he was replaying these events -- but in my own thick mind, I still did not comprehend what that point was.

As the scenes unfolded, some passed ever so fleetingly -- others played out in what seemed like "real" time.

I was an observer and a participant -- it was surreal.

My mind was swirling, swirling.

I saw Annette on our wedding day. She was beautiful. I know they say that all brides are beautiful, but Annette-Oh-How gorgeous! Look at her with those dark Gypsy eyes. Full of youthful innocence, exuberance and the glow of love.

More swirling. I was getting dizzier and dizzier.

There I was standing on 98th Street in Rockaway Beach -- one block from the Boardwalk. I was 4 years old and throwing a tantrum. I wanted chocolate ice cream and my father brought back vanilla. After walking several blocks and waiting in line for the ice cream, he found out that the chocolate was all sold out. He bought the vanilla and my thanks was a tantrum. Next thing I knew the vanilla ice cream was dripping from my nose. My father who never ever chastised me and was the most patient person I ever knew had pushed the ice cream in my face. Boy did I look funny -- though at the time I was far from smiling.

More swirling -- getting faster. I began to lose all sense of balance.

Now I could see the city of Naples as our ship approached the port. Annette and I held hands. Tears welled up in our eyes. How beautiful. This was the land of our ancestors. It was obvious that our area of East New York, Brooklyn had been designed by our grandparents to recreate their homeland.

Swirling -- blurred vision -- nausea -- this was going way too fast.

There was Brother Albert teaching General Science class. While he was lecturing, I was whispering something to my friend, Joe. Brother Albert looked at me and said, "Mr. Colantuoni --you want to be outstanding?"

Well of course I did -- so I quickly

stopped my little sidebar and said, 'Sure.'

"Well you can be outstanding in the hallway." With those few words, he escorted me out the classroom door.

This rush has got to stop -- I'm speeding though my whole life.

Next, Joseph, Annette and I were watching the Fourth of July fireworks from the White House lawn.

More swirling -- it's out of control.

I closed my eyes and I was sitting in Trevi Square, Rome with Annette.

This trip celebrated our love and 30 years of marriage. When we entered the square, we saw a pastry store that also sold gelato -- the smooth creamy Italian ice cream. We shared a gelato and then purchased two glasses of house red wine from a sidewalk café.

We took our wine and sat at the edge of the fountain. I looked in the water and saw that the bottom was covered with coins. I could discern a variety of coin sizes, denominations and countries of origin. We searched our pockets and found two coins. We each took one, made a wish and flipped them into the fountain base. Here we were in the Eternal City -- celebrating an Eternal Love. There were hundreds of tourists and locals in the square at that time but they all blurred into the background and there was just us two. The legend has it that those who throw coins in the fountain will one day return to Rome. I prayed that we will.

The speed intensified -- I was out of control.

And then suddenly with an abruptness that was startling, I came to a jarring halt.

_____

It was November 9, 1977 -- the day started out like the other thousand days since I began working for the Feds.

Annette and I drove in from Queens to Manhattan on the Belt Parkway in our 1973 gold Plymouth Gold Duster. Annette dropped me off at 26 Federal Plaza and then drove back over the Brooklyn Bridge to the Longshoremen's Clinic on Court and Union Streets. Our usual plan was for me to call Annette when I knew what time I would quit and she would drive over the Bridge, pick me up, and then I would do the driving to Queens.

On this day, our plan would not be completed and our lives would change forever.

It was about 5:15 PM.

I was working closely with my boss

Rudy when the call came in for me. It was Annette.

> 'Hey baby, what's up?'
> "Now don't get excited Joe but my water broke."
> 'What? You're not supposed to have the baby until January 20.'
> "Yeah -- I called my doctor and he wants me to meet him at the hospital -- can you get here as soon as possible?"
> 'Of course Babe, I'm on my way.'
> "He doesn't want me to drive so I'll get a ride and leave the car here for you."
> 'Ok, I'll get there as soon as I can.'

I began to feel myself melting into the desk chair and would have fallen to the ground if Rudy had not grabbed me. I shook myself and regained some composure.

By the time I met up with Annette, she

had been admitted to the hospital.

She remained in the hospital 5 more days. During that time, we prayed for our unborn child and each other.

Finally on the fifth day, because the doctors felt that our baby's lungs were mature enough and also to avoid any possibility of infection, they induced labor.

I stayed with Annette as long as they would let me.

Eventually, they rolled her away from me. I stood watching as the gurney that carried my soul mate and my unborn child vanished behind two swinging doors.

The Medivac was ready to take our child away if need be to another hospital.
And I waited -- with the rest of my family.

And I waited for what seemed the long-est wait of my 29 years.

Then the doctor came out and said An-nette was fine -- and so was my son.

My son!!!

A short while later, the two swinging doors that had swallowed up my An-nette swung open again.

I jumped up and ran to see who was on the mobile hospital bed. It was Annette and she was awake.

Her hair was matted down and she ap-peared pale but she had not looked this beautiful to me since our wedding day.

I ran to her and grabbed her hand. She turned to me and smiled.

'I told you I would give you a boy', was the first thing she said.

The Surfmaster waved his arm and said.

"Everything worked out as it was supposed to."

'I was so worried.'

"I know you were -- you always are."

'We were just starting -- I loved her so much -- I love her so much.'

"Do you think that your worrying helps anything or anybody? Don't answer that. Just let me know, how is Joe today?"

'He's fine -- he's about 6 feet tall and weighs about 180 pounds -- and he's got a heart of gold.'

"No thanks to you."

'What do you mean? I've always been a good dad!'

"Sure you have – you've done everything for your children but -- hopefully before today's over you'll get it. It was not your worrying that helped. It was because it was meant to be."

I felt a little disoriented so I sat down on the sand. As my body touched the sand, I could feel the warmth of the earth radiating up through my whole body. The apprehension that had started to grow in my chest began to subside.

_____

The Surfmaster touched my forehead and I could see that I was back to November 30, 2004.

I was in the doctor's waiting room with my dad and mom. My dad had been complaining about aches in his bones. He appeared to be slowing down a bit. He still looked about 10-15 years younger than his 84 years. And his mind and ideas were as sharp as ever.

Many times I said,
'Dad, you're just getting old -- I've got aches too.'
He'd smile and say no more.

We were called in to the doctor's office. I was surprised how young this doctor looked. Even with the youthful appearance, she exuded an air of understanding and compassion. She asked us to sit down and appeared to be searching for the right words to begin talking to us.

"Well, the results of your tests are in Mr. Colantuoni -- and I'm afraid the news is really not that good."

That's how she started and I could see that she was struggling with the information that she had to disclose to us.

She continued, "Your bone scan results are back and it appears that the cancer has spread to your bones."

With that statement, the breath was punched right out of my body. The cancer had spread to the bones? How ill was my dad?

My dad said, "So what are we going to do, Doc?"
"Well there are a few things we can try. I'd like to refer you to a radiologist who deals with this kind of metastasis. I'll call and set up an appointment with him for next week."
"Ok let's try it."

I turned to my mom and saw the horror in her face. She understood what was happening.

Had my dad?

We walked back to the car.

Over the next four weeks, my father got weaker and weaker. He tried the radiation but it was too late. We made six visits to the emergency room with one problem or another. He was dying but I could not face it. Throughout this time, my dad kept his dignity, sense of humor and love for his family.

On his last trip to the Emergency Room on New Year's Eve, dad was still the epitome of what is good about mankind. He had been failing. His color was sallow. The cancer was winning. Undoubtedly his internal organs were being ravaged.

As we returned from the hospital in the

early hours of New Years Day, he still wanted to climb the short flight of stairs and with very little assistance from me, he did.

When we entered his house, I helped him with his coat. He turned to Annette and me and with tear glistened eyes said, "Thank you."

I could hardly muster enough strength to speak but somehow I did, 'No problem -- this is what family's are for -- don't worry, you'll get better, I'm counting on it.'

With these words, my mother, Annette and I helped him to the bedroom -- the room he would never leave.
We called our daughter Amanda. She realized from the tone of my voice that her grandfather's condition was very serious. Within a few hours she arrived with her fiancé Chad to see Grandpa.

Though my dad was beginning to float

in and out of consciousness, when Amanda went in to see him, he recognized her.

> "Hey baby -- How are you?"
> "Fine Grandpa -- you need to get better so you can dance with Grandma at our wedding in April."
> "I'll try baby but I'm feeling pretty tired now."
> "Why don't you rest Grandpa? You know I love you."

He looked into her eyes, smiled and drifted off.

Two days later, he finished his transition to the afterlife. We were lucky enough to have a wonderful young priest give my dad the final blessing right before he drifted away to heaven. The priest stayed with us and consoled us.

We made arrangements to move him to

New York where we buried him with his siblings.

The Surfmaster lightly patted my hand and I was again on the beach with him.

"So how do you feel?"

"I still miss him"

"I know you do but do you remember the poem you wrote after your dad's funeral?

'You mean "The Flow"?'

"Yes, I inspired you to write those words."

'You did? Why?'

"I was trying to make you understand what you needed to do -- your dad always knew this and tried to teach you. You searched your whole life for a guru -- you had lived with him and never realized it. Why don't you read over the words to that poem? If I remember correctly after you finished writing it, you folded it up and put it in your wallet."

Even though I did not remember putting it there, when I opened my wallet, I found a folded piece of paper. I took it out, unfolded it and began to read these words.

_____

The Flow

Why do I continue to try?
Why don't I let things go by?
Whether I'm high or low
I just cannot find the Flow

So many days I tried
So many days I cried
Why didn't I know?
You have to stay with the Flow

There is much you can earn
Even more you can learn
If you let yourself go
And get into the Flow

If I continue to love
And with some help from above
My soul will continue to grow
And then I will be the Flow

I began shaking my head. Why was this happening?

The Surfmaster looked at me and saw that I was still puzzled and confused.

"I want you to see another section from your life."

With that he tapped me on my right shoulder and my eyes closed gently.

In my minds eye it was April 9, 2005. My baby, Amanda, was getting married.

The buildup to this day had been exciting and nerve wracking. From what I understood preparations for weddings get crazier as you get closer to the big day. There was an added stressor during this time.

Annette was having more and more issues with her aortic valve. She had been born with a faulty valve but it had only been an issue the last couple of years.

But in late 2004, the doctor said her condition had deteriorated. A year before, her case was considered mild but now it was severe. Would she even be able to walk down the aisle as the matron of honor?

I wanted her to take care of herself but she always allowed other issues to take precedence over her own health. First, it was my dad's health. He was dying and Annette did not want to put her needs before my dad's.

On the way home from my dad's funeral, Annette started to have an attack. We rushed her to the hospital and they admitted her. They stabilized her and then released her.

Once again I wanted her to take care of herself. Once again she thought of others. She did not want to mess up Amanda's wedding or the planning for it. I was worried that she would not make it to the wedding. I was worried that something would happen to her and that the flame of the love of my life would be extinguished.

I watched her while she was awake. I stared at her while she was asleep. I lived in constant fear that she was not going to make it.

The Surfmaster interjected,

> "Well did she?"
> 'You know quite well she did!'
> "And the wedding?"
> 'Like a wonderful fairy tale -- in fact Amanda called the day after to say the wedding and the party that followed were better than she even hoped for. She then thanked Annette and me and told us that she loved us.'
> "It all worked out"

'Yes it did.'
"That's right -- in spite of you."

———————————

With a slight wave of his hand, the Surfmaster brought me back to now. We were again standing on the beach. The winds had picked up slightly and there were more whitecaps on the water.

'How did you do that?'

"Wrong question Joe -- why did I do that? With me all things are possible."

'So then why?'

"I wanted you to understand some basic truths."

'Well I think I got it -- you're always around, right?'

"That's for sure but anything else?"

'No matter how hard you try -- things will work out for the best if you don't get in the way.'

"Even if you don't realize it at the time -- what was that you said?"

'You have to stay in the Flow.'

"That's it Joe -- and now you're

beginning to understand the why -- Why did I come here? -- Because there are more basics to learn -- And why now? Because I knew you would get it this time. I need to show you something and then I will share with you those ingredients you need to cultivate for yourself and the sake of the entire world."

With this last comment, I noticed that the Surfmaster was no longer just a Surfmaster.

He was radiant -- jagged bolts of light encircled his entire body and emanated from his fingers. His countenance was peaceful and beautiful. He shone greater than the brightest stars in the sky.

He raised both hands into the sky. He closed his eyes and his lips were moving.

A strange sensation started in my body. Goose bumps appeared on my arms and the hairs on my neck began to tingle. Then I realized what was happening. There was no wind blowing -- there was a surreal quiet over the beach. When I looked at the ocean, I could not believe my eyes.

The water was still -- there was absolutely no wave action. The entire surface of the water glistened in the sun with a metallic sparkle. It looked as if I could walk on this glistening surface.

If there was any doubt who the Surfmaster really was up until then, there was no doubt any longer.

_____

He put out his hand.

"Joe walk with me."

I placed my hand in his and we walked. We turned toward the ocean and continued walking.

It was unbelievable -- we were walking on top of the ocean -- I turned to look at the Surfmaster and he said,

"Joe, look at the horizon -- that's our destination -- Do not waiver!"

I remembered the story of St. Peter and his walk on the water and what happened when his faith faltered. He started to sink.

I trusted the Surfmaster and turned ahead, I felt a peace engulfing me that I had never felt before. I knew that I was safe. The sky was the most beautiful shade of blue that I had ever seen. Right in front of my eyes I saw the most beautiful rainbow develop. It started developing at the north east corner of the horizon. The colors began to unfurl as the rainbow ascended to its apex and continued like the most colorful of carpets through its descent to the south. A carpet fit for royalty could not have been more beautiful.

As soon as the arc of the rainbow was complete, a second arc began to develop just beneath the first rainbow. This smaller rainbow fit completely below the first and contained an even more intense panoply of colors.

We continued walking -- and my sense of peace continued to grow. Through all this I kept my sites on the horizon.

I began to notice a smell. It seemed familiar but at first I could not recognize it.

It was faintly metallic but also a bit sweet and spicy. What was it? It made me feel more comfortable and at peace.

I racked my brain to decipher the smell -- the more I tried to figure it out, the more frustrated I became.

What a dunce! Didn't I just learn that you had to get into the Flow? -- forcing things never worked. When the time was right and if I was open to the knowledge, I'd know what the smell was.

So we continued walking. I was enraptured by the sheer beauty of the moment.

It was then that I began to remember the smell. When I would kiss my children goodbye in the mornings on my way to work, the smell of my aftershave would stay on their pillows. They called that the Daddy Smell. We often joked about it as they grew up.

This was the Daddy Smell but different. When my dad came home from working over night on the sheet metal machines, his clothing smelled just like that metallic smell -- and that sweet/spice smell was Old Spice, my dad's after shave.

I glimpsed to my side and the Surfmaster was no longer there -- next to me, holding my hand was my dad.

He looked at me with those large brown eyes and all I could see was love.

"You know you always made me proud", he said.

And just like it was the most natural thing in the world to begin talking to my dead dad, I said,

'I know dad -- but did you know how much I loved and respected you?'

"Sure I did."

'You look great.'

"Well I am now free of the ravages of the cancer and my spirit is alive with love and hope."

'Have you kept up with what has happened since you left?'

"Sure I know about Annette's operation, Mandy's wedding and how good Joe-Joe's doing. These are all great. I was with you through all of these times."

'I know I often felt you -- but I thought I was losing my mind.'

"Why Joe, I would have expected with all that you have read you would have been prepared for such spiritual encounters!"

'You're right dad -- I should have been -- but you know sometimes you want something so bad that you can not believe it's really happening when it is.'

"Sure -- I know what you mean -- but you know I'm a little con- cerned about your mom."

'You know dad how stubborn she can be.'

"Sure I do and loved every minute of it -- you know I really loved her and did not want to leave her -- but I had to -- it was my time -- she has to keep living while she can -- she still has much to offer to you, your family and others -- there is a time when we will be together again -- it's just not now, it's just not yet -- tell her I love her still and will be waiting for her when it is her time."

At this point, the Surfmaster appeared ahead of us -- right at the horizon line.

Once again he raised his arms and his lips moved. He then pointed his arm at the horizon and traced the shape of a door on the horizon. He put out his right hand and pulled open a doorway -- a doorway!!

We continued walking and then stepped into the doorway and through the threshold.

On the other side of the doorway was an alternate world.

My dad turned to go.

'Please dad stay some more with me.'
"Joe, you need to do this on your

own but remember, I'll always be there for you if you need me. If you feel alone, remember -- I'm there. If you feel unloved, remember -- I love you. And if you need me -- just talk to me -- I will answer you -- I will be with you always as you are with me."

With these words, he hugged and kissed me and walked away.

———————————

As I began walking through the alternate world, I noticed that it was populated with all kinds of people.

There was a similarity to my world but there was also something different. What was it?

I heard the voice of the Surfmaster,

> "This world is the world of Wonderful Possibilities. This is how reality would be if everyone stayed in the Flow.
> All is possible if the Flow is considered. Everything will be right and at the right time if you are sensitive to the full universe of possibilities.
> Happiness, peace and love are all possible if you want them enough. You have to choose these positive feelings."

The Surfmaster came up behind me and touched my shoulder and said,

"What do you think?"

'This is all so amazing', I said.

"Would you like to explore some more?"

'I sure would.'

"I'll give you some more time and check back with you in a little while -- you must remember one thing -- this is the World of Possibilities -- it is how I wanted your world to be -- it is a potential world -- you cannot directly interact with anyone or anything you see -- you will be able to move around at will -- just think of where you want to go and you will be there. But remember potential only becomes real when it is acted upon. You can activate this reality when you get back to your world -- see you in a bit."

With that he walked off and left me to observe this alternative reality.

_____

While I explored, I noticed that the people in this alternate world appeared to be smiling most of the time. The urban areas were crowded but I could not see any garbage strewn streets or sidewalks. Single family homes and apartments in the inner city all looked brighter and fresher than those in the world I just left.

As I progressed, through rural areas, I was immediately struck by the vibrancy and lushness of the plants and vegetation.

I looked over someone's shoulder at the newspaper he was reading. There were no stories of murder, rape or war. Instead there were glowing tributes to the goodness and the potential of the human race.

I wanted to talk to the Surfmaster. I needed to ask him what I was really witnessing. Why had he shown me this world, when I lived in one that was so screwed up?

As if reading my mind, the Surfmaster appeared at my side.

I asked him,

> 'Why does this world appear so peaceful and full of love?'
> "As I have said, what you have seen is the reality that I intended for all people. The world that you came from could be as love filled, if you want."
> 'Of course, I want that -- but how?
> "That Joe is the main reason, I came to you these last two days -- to show you what was necessary. Your world can be full of love and peace."
> 'I don't get it. What's stopping us?'

"You are!"
'Me?'
"And all those who do not under-
stand a few simple truths."

I blinked my eyes and when I reopened them the Surfmaster and I were back on the beach.

I could feel the breeze on my face again. As I looked out over the water, I could see the undulations of the ocean as it renewed its eternal assault on the shore line.

I looked to the left and I saw the Surfmaster.

Why had he shown me a replay of all those times of my life? Why had I seen my dad?
Was this the moment I had read about in so many novels? The moment before my death -- the moment when a per-

son's whole earthly existence passes in front of them.

Quite unexplainably, I was not tense or anxious but filled with serenity. I felt at peace!

I saw a seagull soaring through the cobalt blue sky. As it gained altitude, it caught an upper air current and began to glide gracefully. With what appeared to be no effort at all, the gull arched its body and began what appeared to be a tightly choreographed aerial dance. This dance ended with the gull diving towards the water and ever so slightly touching the surface of the ocean. Once the gull came to rest, it seamlessly became one with the ocean surface. As the waves gently rolled toward the beach, the gull rolled up and down on the wave crests. I wanted to be that gull -- I wanted to possess that same ability to soar and drift in harmony. But I began to believe that my time on this planet was up. The Surfmaster had let me see a life review -- my next step would be death.

Exactly at the moment these thoughts were formulating in my brain, the Surfmaster spoke up,

"No, Joe you are not dying -- at least not yet, not now -- I want to explain the truths I mentioned before."

———————————

THE SIMPLE TRUTHS

As the sunlight began to cast shadows on the sand perpendicular to our bodies, the Surfmaster took two steps back. It was difficult to determine what shone brighter -- the orb in the sky responsible for lighting and heating our world or the countenance of the Surfmaster.

The sparkle in his eyes was hypnotic. He bowed to each direction of the compass. Then he extended his arms straight out and raised his palms up over his head. As his hands passed his face, he raised his eyes upwards and once again I could see his mouth moving. I could not make out what he was saying. He then lowered his arms and looked directly at me. He took two steps towards me and stopped.

"Humans are the noblest of creatures. It was originally intended that everyone live in happiness and peace just like the alternate world you observed.

Joe, you have done pretty well when it comes to all the 'Thou shall nots' -- even though you came pretty close to crossing the line on a few of them.

But it is now time to go further, for you to understand that love and peace are possible if you really want them. Each person has the innate ability to achieve them but most often do not. This requires you to DO something -- not just 'not' do something.

I have visited you so I can help you. I ask that you impart this knowledge to your family and friends. They in turn should pass these ideas on. Trust me when I say even though what I will teach you will create benefits for the world -- many will find fault with you and what you say.

Some because they will not believe how simple the solution is. Others because they believe the way the world is progressing gives them an advantage. Still others have even more sinister motives.

As I said earlier, human beings were created to be happy. I have watched you over many years and believe that you have a good heart. You are the ripple that at some point will be a tidal wave. I have a lot of faith in what a few dedicated people can accomplish."

The Surfmaster had faith in me?

I felt a wave of energy growing in me. If he felt that I might have a chance at making a difference, I would do all I could. As my mind began to envision how I would proceed, the Surfmaster asked me to move closer so he could begin my lesson.

"It's very simple, Joe! In fact, the simplicity is one of the reasons that most people have not figured out how to make planet earth the place I envisioned.

People tend to create complexity where it need not exist. They believe that the secrets of life are contained in complex chemical formula or DNA chains. The more complicated they make things, the further they are from discovering what is out there in the open for all to see.

Please take these ideas and understand the intent -- peace and happiness. Do not make them more than they are -- they are the means -- not the end.

Do not fret or get anxious over what I tell you. And please no guilt on what has happened in the past. As they said in the 60's -- today is the first day of the rest of your life.

Are you ready?"

'As ready as I ever will be.'

"Ok -- lets talk -- you need to understand it's not about who wins."

"That's right, Joe. It really is not about who wins. I know this appears to go against human nature but maybe that is exactly why it's important.

Let me give you an example of what I mean -- two people are having a discussion on just about any topic you can imagine. At some point, their ideas begin to diverge. As the divergence grows, so grows each of their need to justify why their path is the right one. If necessary, each one will fight and get ugly to 'win' the point.

This plays out with married couples, business partners and nations.

Every encounter -- be it a conversation or a diplomatic negotiation -- need not be conducted with the result of there being a winner or a loser. It's OK to compromise.

Differences are alright. Situations

sometimes must be left to just 'Be'.

If you are victorious, how long are you happy?

If you are vanquished, how long are you sad?

None of the trauma or bad will are necessary.

Some people talk louder to get their point across -- to win. Others use sarcasm or other forms of verbal cruelty to win.

The amount of hurt and evil generated by this obsession to win has often caused people to act less nobly than they were intended to act. You must always respect the dignity of others.

Joe, just think about the last time you had a discussion with someone -- remember how as the conversation progressed, you became more and more invested in the outcome of the discussion. So much so that you felt that you had to make your point. On those occasions when your point was made, how did you feel?"

'Great.'

"How long did you feel 'great'?"

'Oh, I don't know…'

"I do -- not long at all. In fact, if you are honest with yourself, the effort to 'win' is never worth the paltry prize -- a moment at best of half-baked self satisfaction."

'But suppose you are in a discussion or a relationship with someone who does not understand this -- what do you do if they keep pushing and nudging to be right? How do you deal with that? I'm not sure I can.'

"Joe, it's simple but not easy! You need to practice. You will get it and so hopefully will those who you deal with when they see how you change.

You must not forget that winning at all costs is no win at all. If you allow for differences and no one gets hurt, so what? Those around you will begin to take a more peaceful approach to all they do.

Now there are certain basic issues that you can not equivocate about or do not fall into the area where the win is not important. And Joe you know these -- you know issues concerning the preservation and sanctity of life. Think of life as my gift and not something to be marketed or dealt with as a relative commodity.

And sure I'd like to win a World Series, a Superbowl or some such things -- for the fun of it -- but remember not at all costs and certainly not if the win gets in the way of fulfilling the reality you deserve.

Now, if you agree and realize that this obsessive desire to win clouds almost all your human interactions you will begin to understand what I'm suggesting.

When you realize this, you start to know what needs to be done to create the reality I always intended for this world.

As you learn to be less confrontational, you must also practice forgiveness. It is only through forgiveness that people can begin to heal. As individual people heal, so will the world."

_____

"So are you with me, Joe?"

'Yeah, so far so good -- I see how an obsessive need to win points can detract from my happiness and that I need to practice forgiving more -- yeah -- I'm good with those ideas.'

"Ok, before we move on, I was wondering if you were thirsty or hungry?"

I was exhausted and exhilarated at the same time. I could use something to drink after a day like today.

'Sure, I'll have something to drink -- what do you have?'

"When I come to the shore, I am usually pretty stocked -- beer or wine?"

'I'll try some wine -- red if you have?'

"Sure do, I'm partial myself to red wine."

When he said this, I noticed a twinkle in his eye.

He opened a huge, unmarked jug.

He took out a large plastic goblet and filled it with a clear ruby-red liquid. He pushed the goblet to me and poured himself one.

We touched glasses in a silent toast. I raised my drink towards my lips. A deliciously intoxicating aroma rose from my glass and into my nose. Soon, I was suffused with the freshness and intensity of the brew. I had never tasted a better wine or a wine that so quickly enraptured me. This feeling of exhilaration spread. Every cell of my body was being infused with a warm glow.

"Joe, let's continue -- we can talk while we drink."

_____

"Joe, you need to understand that everyday is a gift. When you wake up in the morning (if you are fortunate enough to sleep) you need to say 'Thank you'.

With each new day, comes all the possibilities you need to be happy. As the sun rises, so should your hope and expectations that peace and love will prevail.

I often say -- You need to seize the day, the moment and all the possibilities included in the universe. The Romans said 'carpe diem'.

Make the most of all that I provide. When you take those first fresh breaths of a new day, include a blessing that this day be wonderful and full -- that it bears out its potential to be the beginning of unlimited wonder.

I'm sure, Joe, you've heard of many people who put off doing

something or experiencing something and then regret that decision.
I also know that you have known
people who have postponed doing
things that they wanted to do their
whole lives only to tragically die
while they waited for the right
moment.

Remember -- this is not a dress
rehearsal!"

What did he just say? Didn't Annette's
friend Becky always say that?

'Wait a minute -- Annette's friend
Becky has been saying the same
thing since we met her.'

"Who do you think told Becky?"

'You did? Did you appear to her
too?'

"I'm not always this flamboyant.
Sometimes I'm subtle. I can be
that hunch that you get. Or I
could be that quiet voice pushing
you to try something. I came to
you this way to make sure you did

not miss the rest of your life and its limitless potential.

Often I overhear debates about whether or not there is life after death. Who are they kidding? To them I say -- OF COURSE THERE IS! That's why I allowed you to talk to your dad -- to show you that there is an afterlife. I think people need to be more concerned with what they do with the life before death and let me worry about the life after!

You can not be so preoccupied with what will happen in the future that you neglect to enjoy my gift to you -- that's right, it's called the present because it's the now and it's my gift to all. Remember what your friend, Father Tom says, 'Yesterday is History, Tomorrow is Mystery, But Today is Reality; Live It."

_____

"Joe, you see that I work through many different people and in many different ways. Goodness and learning are all around you. When I look into your heart and mind, I see that you are starting to get it and that's good. I now want to work <u>through</u> you. So let's continue because there are just a few more things I'd like to cover."

I was glowing with new found hope. The Surfmaster had looked inside me, knew that I was catching on and wanted to work through me.

"Well let's continue, OK?"

I nodded.

"OK, then you must believe that I want the best for you. The world, the universe and all that exists are there to help you with whatever you need. The trick is you need to be open to the limitless potential that I have created for you. It's all there if you look. It's all there if as you said earlier, you get into the Flow.

You need to sensitize yourself to the fact that nothing happens by chance. There is a reason for everything and the reason is to promote the good -- but most times you do not understand because you are not sensitive or ready to grasp the meaning.

With me, there are all possibilities. You need to understand that. You need not grasp everything to understand that there is a plan. Just believe.

You know that the harder you try to accomplish something, it usually slips further and further away. You are at your best when you don't overtry. Remember when you used to bowl on Sunday mornings?"

'Sure -- that seems like a thousand years ago!'

"You did your best when you were loose -- you didn't pull the release -- you got into the zone and you did pretty well.

Now I know some of those times were right after you had a little too much partying on the night before. So, I'm not recommending unlimited alcohol use -- what I am reminding you of is this -- when you went naturally or in the Flow -- you were so much more effective than when you tried too hard.

Goodness is the natural order and the way I intended all things to be -- we just need to remind people of that."

"Still with me?"

'I'm just amazed at how simple you are making this seem!'

"It's the simplicity that tricks everyone up -- you ok to continue?"

'Please.'

"You must take stock of what is around you. Remember that Enough is Enough. I have provided sufficient quantities of everything necessary for people to live. Yet, there is hunger, sickness and a weakening environment. How can this be? Simple -- man is a hoarder. And there is really no need for this. Enough is Enough. At dinner feasts -- how much do you really need to eat? Or how many clothes do you need to own? How large does your house have to be?

I am not saying that you should not want to look nice, or live in a nice place or even eat gourmet food.

No, I am really talking about excess and I know that you've seen what I mean -- people have to realize that too much stuff gets in the way of a person getting into the Flow.

Stuff weighs you down and creates all kinds of worry and anxiety. Simplify. Appreciate. Remember you can't take it with you. And if you really think about it -- stuff deteriorates, ages and breaks. You never see a U-Haul following a hearse. Only love and the soul live on.

Try to do good -- good things, good words, and good thoughts. It's not enough to just do no harm. Wars have been fought, people have been killed and families torn apart because some people value material possessions more than they value love and peace.

If you look back, how many wars in the past have been fought to get

economic advantage over someone? The "haves" versus the
"have nots". With no one winning.
You have seen brother and sister
or sister and sister turn on each
other to gain materials that will
surely deteriorate as fast as a
chunk of ice on a summer day.

For sure you need to be clothed,
fed and sheltered. But do none of
these at the expense of your
neighbor or even more tragically
your family.

The worst cancer that has ever entered the human body is the cancer
called selfishness. There is no
known cure for it except a radical
excision of the sick person's val-
ues, thoughts and beliefs.

Think of others -- that will be the
most beneficial thought for you."

"Well Joe, it comes down to this -- happiness is an inherited and an acquired trait. You are born to it but you must choose it, daily.

The main difference between a happy person and a sad person is attitude. Sure, events can precipitate certain feelings but it's the way you interpret the event that determines where you are on the spectrum between happiness and sadness.

Let's talk about something that we all experience at one time or another -- death. If you believe that I have even more in store for you than this earthly existence, the sadness of losing someone is ameliorated. Sure you miss them, sure you are sorry that you can't see them, hug them, love them or be loved by them as you did when they lived. But if you have witnessed a debilitating illness, you must learn to be happy that the person is no longer suffering.

If someone leaves your earth earlier than you had wanted them to, you must trust that I have a better understanding of what that person needs than you do.

Let's move to what you experience on a daily basis. Every time you perceive your world, you have two choices -- you can appreciate what is there and be happy or you can complain and be sad. Every moment of every day of your life, you can determine if you are happy.

And if you are not happy -- do not blame me -- change your thoughts. Have you noticed that people in what you might consider the worst of circumstances can be happy? Look you will see.

Happiness is a matter of you believing you are.

You still with me, Joe?"

'This is a little tougher but I'm

getting it.'

"Good, I thought you would.

Ok -- its now time for me to gather up my gear and leave you. Remember what we've spoken about -- and that I love you and have more patience than the most patient person you have ever known."

I wanted to spend more time with the Surfmaster. His presence had filled me with love and the belief that there really was a better tomorrow for everyone. I asked him if he could stay just a little longer.

He said,

> "Joe, I think it's time -- and remember I have been with you since before you were born and will always be there -- loving you and in your corner. It's now up to you. I want you to go and spread these words far and wide. The future depends on you doing as I have taught you."

With these challenging words, he started walking towards the sand dune. Even though I still wanted him to stay, I believed that he would be there for me as I needed him.

I turned to watch the Surfmaster as he left. I saw from the side of my eye a shadow begin to pass next to me. I turned my head to the side and I saw the largest flock of seagulls that I had ever seen. They were moving from east to west -- going from the ocean to inland. There were so many that they appeared as a dark cloud, blocking the rays of the sun. As each of these graceful birds landed near where the Surfmaster was walking, I noticed a startling transfor-mation. Where each bird touched down, there now was a tall stately oth-erworldly winged figure. These figures bowed to the Surfmaster and sur-rounded him. Over the roar of the surf and the bustle of the wind, I could just make out the sound of what I thought was a chant.

The Surfmaster and his winged devo-tees moved in unison until they were beyond my field of sight. I got up to run towards them but as I approached where they were, I could see that they were there no more.

I looked around and heard the bustle of people enjoying this glorious day.

My head was surprisingly clear. My senses were finely tuned. I breathed the ocean air and was able to discern a plethora of aromas -- all of which added to the intensity of the moment. I possessed a new clarity of vision. Colors were more vibrant. I was experiencing life in a new dimension.

I began walking south at the beach line. I looked intently at each person I passed. When our eyes made contact, a new connection was established. Smiles appeared. I believed that I could accomplish what the Surfmaster wanted.

I stepped into the VW and started to think. How was I going to tell Annette what had happened? What words could I use to describe this miraculous day? I prayed that when I began to speak to her, the Surfmaster would help provide me the right words.

I drove west on 136th Street and stopped at the light on Coastal. Since this was the off-season, the east-west lights did not change as fast as they did during the height of the season. But it didn't bother me like it had just a few hours ago.

The light changed and I continued on 136th until my driveway. I was pleasantly surprised to see a silver Bug in the driveway -- that meant Amanda and Chad were visiting.

I got out of the car, walked up the stairs and opened the door. My family was talking more animatedly than usual. There they were Annette, Joe, Amanda, Chad and my mom.

As I walked towards them, in unison they stopped talking and turned in my direction. The expressions on their face ranged from startled to relieved.

Before any of them could say anything, I said,

> 'So what's up? Whatcha all doing here? How did I get so lucky to get all the people I love together?'

Annette was the first to speak up,

> "Where have you been? We've been worried about you!"
> 'I'm fine.'
> "What happened to your face?"

With that I looked in the dining room mirror and saw that my face was burnt - - as if I had been too close to a sunlamp.

My hair which had been turning gray was now snow white.

'I need to tell you all what happened on the beach. It's the best news that I could tell you.'

With what I knew was the help of the Surfmaster, I proceeded to recount the events that had transpired. Not one of my beloved even thought to question what was being said. They all sat in awe. Annette squeezed my hand to reassure me of her love.

I could see that my story had affected them. There was a sense of wonder and delight in the air. I told them that I was a bit bushed and wanted to take a short nap. We planned to go to Happy Hour and have some steamed shrimp. We needed to discuss how to begin the work that the Surfmaster wanted us to accomplish.

As I lay down in bed, I knew that my

life would never be the same and that tomorrow would be the beginning of the new world.

I closed my eyes and saw the Surfmaster smiling at me and giving me the thumbs up sign. He was surrounded by his winged companions. I then knew that the future might be rocky and with some problems but things were going to be all right.

———————————

DEDICATION

I hope you enjoyed the story of the Surfmaster. If it makes you rethink past moments in your life, I wish that you learn whatever teachings were placed there for you.

I believe that we all have had brushes with the Divine but are usually too pre-occupied to realize it. For those who do not remember their last encounter, I pray that your own Surfmaster visit you soon. We need this help if we are to overcome the evils in the world -- the war, hatred, and hunger.

I believe that we will get this help if we ask. If we follow the advice of the Surfmaster, there is no room for terror-ism, murder and neglect.

I want to thank all my friends -- those who I have known for many years and those that I have recently met. You all know what you mean to me.

I want to thank God for opening my eyes to His Wonder and for giving me the most supportive and loving family.

I want to thank my parents -- my mom and my dad (who left this earthly existence last year) for their love and example.

I want to thank my children -- Joseph and Amanda (and Chad her husband) for their continued love and affection.

And my Annette -- she has been a partner in the ups and downs of our life together. If we were to have an immortal existence here on earth, it still would not be enough time to spend with her. I am so glad that I know that there is more than just this earthly existence. We will be able to share our love in eternity.

Look into your hearts and you will see that if you practice what the Surfmaster suggests, your life and the lives of those around you will improve. May you all have the good fortune to know and be in communion with your own Surfmaster on a daily basis.

Peace
Love
JC

Special thanks to Amanda and Chad for their help in editing, Annette for her great cover illustration, the suggestions/advice from Andrea Schlottman and Pat McDonnell from the Worcester County Library and to my spiritual advisor and friend, Father Thomas J. Protack for his critiques, suggestions and friendship.

Printed in the United States
4808 ILVS00001B/205-303